How to Change your Life: Self Improvement, Progress, Get Healthy, Fit, Make More Money, & Create a Better Life

By Colby Meyier

Copyright 2019
Third Edition, License Notes

Copyright Info:

Legal Info:

Preface

We want to take a moment to say thank you for purchasing our guide online. HiddenStuff Entertainment remains one of the top app and eBook publishers online. It is our commitment to bring you the most important information to enrich your life.

We sincerely hope that you find this guide useful and beneficial in your quest for betterment. We want to provide readers with knowledge and build their skills to perform at the highest levels within their topics of interest. This in turn contributes to a positive and more enjoyable experience. After all, it is our belief that things in life are to be enjoyed as much as they possibly can be.

If you are in need of additional support or resources in regards to this guide, please feel free to visit our webpage at Hiddenstuffentertainment.com

Contents

How to Change your Life: Self Improvement, Progress, Get Healthy, Fit, Make More Money, & Create a Better Life.............1

Preface...4

Introduction..6

Slow down...7

Be prepared to change...8

Accept responsibility..9

Know your best values..10

Know your cause...11

Replace limiting beliefs with empowering beliefs...................12

Replace bad habits with positive habits............................13

Get a mentor...14

Have the right expectation..15

Maintain your momentum...16

Love..17

Exercise...18

Eat Better..19

Habits...21

Goals..22

Conclusion...23

Introduction

Change is essential for growth. You cannot grow if you are static. It is impossible to grow if you refuse to change how you act and think. Hence, a change of life is something that happens continuously. It does not end. The instant you halt your change process, you halt growth.

I'm not saying that I know everything about changing life. I'm still learning myself. But here I'd like to share with you what I have learned so far. I do not know all there is as it concerns changing life. Hence, I am still learning as well. However, I would love to share what I have learnt with thus far.

Have a look at 10 tips for changing your life:

Slow down

Changing your life requires that you stop for a second to think as well as reflect. If you're the type that is busy all the time, you will hardly have time to think of your life; not to talk of taking any steps to force a change. Applying the below tips will be alien to you. Therefore, slow down so you can have time to change.

If you slow down, you will enjoy your life. It is not just the scenery you miss when you go extremely fast – you equally don't catch the sense of your destination.
Eddie Cantor

Be prepared to change

Being willing is absolutely basic. It is your life; no one can do it except you. Should you be unwilling to change, virtually nothing can change you on this planet.

To have a willing heart, you should first realize that it is possible to improve your life from where it is now. Regardless of how beautiful you see your life, there is room for improvement. In stark contrast, do not feel hopeless if you are going through some hard times at the moment. Your life can always be changed positively.

Accept responsibility

Being responsible for a couple of things is also part of the game. Do not go on blaming others for bad experiences you've had. Do not blame, your friends, family, boss or even the economy. Whether you are experiencing ups or downs is all a function of you. The moment you assume your responsibility, you will not be far from real change.

We turn out more effective whenever we decide we are going to change ourselves instead of hoping that things will change for our sakes.
Stephen Covey

Know your best values

In your deepest of hearts, there are a couple of principles you know to be true. Take out time to know them. What's the most significant thing that has life has to offer? What are the principles that ensures a fulfilled life? You should align yourself and thoughts with these values. Find those values and tell yourself about them constantly.

Know your cause

Change has never been easy for anyone, you just need to overcome a certain force to get started. As space shuttles require powerful rocket to go past the gravity of Earth, you equally need a huge amount of energy for overcoming that force that restricts change. Your purpose is your energy source. Your cause is capable of filling you with that strength to go past that inertia. Knowing your cause means knowing what is important to you.

Replace limiting beliefs with empowering beliefs

Limiting beliefs also make for reasons why you find it difficult to change your life. It is essential you identify these beliefs to enable you handle them effectively. To know the limiting beliefs you have, scan your mind and look for phrases such as:

"I can't ..."
"I will always be ..."
"I won't be able to ..."
"There is no way ..."
The moment you find any one of them, scribble it down. After a while, view your list. Those are your own limiting beliefs.

After knowing your own limiting beliefs, they should be replaced with positive beliefs. Write down positive statements which counter the negative thoughts you had scribbled down and then make positive confessions with such statements. Anytime you are confronted with any limiting belief, do it.

Replace bad habits with positive habits

In addition to knowing your own limiting beliefs, it is expected that you know your bad habits. Do you have habits that pull you down? Do you have habits you ought to break out from? Have them all listed.

Instead of thinking of how you can break those habits, think on creating positive habits that can replace those. For instance, let us assume your bad habit has to do with watching TV excessively. Instead of focusing on spending less TV time, consider building habits that use up that time more efficiently. For example, you may consider developing the habit to read.

Get a mentor

Another way to improve your life is by having a mentor. Not only will your mentor help you with important advice in critical situations, they can equally warn of you possible lapses on that path. Without any mentor, it will take you a much longer time to learn most things. Mentors help you save a lot of time.

It is not easy to get a reliable mentor though. In most cases, it is not easy for anyone to invest quality time in you when there is nothing in for them. At least you should appear teachable and open-minded. Moreover, try make yourself relevant to that mentor of yours. Aid him in his work if you can. That way, you are indicating a hard working mentee that's worth the time and energy.

Have the right expectation

Having an ideal expectation from the onset is extremely relevant. Otherwise, you could easily be frustrated when things do not go as you've expected. Change is gradual, particularly when you are after long-term changes. Having realistic expectations prepares your mind for hard times.

Maintain your momentum

The hardest part has always been the starting. The moment you can scale that hurdle, things will begin to fall into place as long as your sustain the momentum. It is like when you push a car. You'd figure that the hardest part is initially moving the car. The moment it starts moving, pushing will no longer be difficult provided you do not allow it stop.

In like manner, keep making your life better. Change the way you do things daily. Similar to the above quote, if you do not change, you do not grow.

Love

A good self-improvement tip to begin with is learning how to love your own self. Unfortunately for majority, this is easier than it sounds. You should accept yourself for who you are, and you are beautiful as you are. Everyone mustn't be a singer like Adele or be an actor like Brad Pitt. Just be yourself.

All though our lives others make us feel bad about ourselves. It is about the things we believe, things we wear or who we see ourselves to be. They're against you. Stand for you and not for them! If you stand against you, it will be hard to living a beautiful life. Learn how to be an ally of yourself and not an enemy to yourself.

Talk to yourself about how unique you are daily. It could be difficult initially, but as you progress it will get easier. Recognize the qualities and talents that make you stand out. And seriously, we all have that special thing inside of us.

This was a tough tip for me. I began by looking at myself inside the mirror while saying to myself that I was great. It was a bit weird. I did not believe it though. However, something funny happened. After going on with this for days, I started believing it. It sounded good and I became more excited doing this every day.

Exercise

I do exercise a couple of times in a week. Anytime I do, it feels great. Working out gives me a positive feeling about who I am and steps up my mood. Therefore, whenever I'm unable to go the gym due to a busy schedule, I end up being less motivated and have a sour mood.

Should you visit the gym and not feel anything, try lifting heavier weights, as that puts your beyond that comfort zone of yours. Many people prefer light because they feel they are able to lift things many times or simply because they are afraid to get bulky and big.

I am telling you, you have the capacity to lift weights you never thought you could lift and you wouldn't become bulky or big, lest it has been grafted in your DNA. I have been doing very heavy weight for over 10 years now. I am not close to being bulky and big.

When you carry heavy weights, more effort is exerted by your body and additional endorphins are sent into your body. This is responsible for making you feel good and enhancing your mood. When you are put through such motions, your body hardly responds since it is not being worked.

Having said that, if you're new to weight lifting, definitely start with something light you do not have yourself injured.

Eat Better

If you want to do workouts, then it becomes essential that you feed well. My eating is better when I work out. Whenever I stop my working out, my eating becomes poor. It is a really simple cycle. I carry weights and I feel great about myself, and I do eat well; the cycle continues.

Many times you feel like crap simply because you eat sugary, highly processed foods. Try eating healthy for one week. Reduce the amount of sugar you take and consume more of natural foods such as vegetables and fruits.

When starting out this is going to be difficult, but your body needs time to make that adjustment. So if you allow it, you would be greatly surprised at the improvement. That energy drop you feel every afternoon will eventually disappear. You will no longer be waking up tired. You only need some days and your body will adjust.

I began with the aim of just consuming more vegetables and fruits. My only goal then was to see how I can take more of this food type.

I included one banana to my diet at breakfast and included some spinach in my eggs. At first I was scared, but you can hardly taste that spinach.

I eat apple as snacks. During lunch as well as dinner, I would include some vegetables. I may not be sure of what the food pyramid calls such foods, but this method worked miracles for me.

Play a bit around it and find out what works for you more. Even when you prefer water over soda, and take your apples instead of doughnuts, you are only going to be helping yourself.

Habits

We are creatures with habits. We observe similar routines on a daily basis. This makes living easy for us, yet equally makes us to be lazy. To add some sparks to your life, you should consider changing your habits. This is not about stopping o brush your teeth, although perhaps brushing with the other hand.

Instead of using one route to your office daily, try another route. Tuesday nights can be your family night. Look for simple ways that can help you change things a bit.

The more your chances of doing this, the higher chances of keeping your body and mind alert, constantly learning. Revisiting the exercise talk, it is a similar idea. If you do not step up the weight you carry, your body will adapt to that exercise and will not be challenged, which means you are not growing.

Another approach to changing your habit is by starting your day on the right note. Learn how you can be a master of your mornings. That will impact the rest part of your day greatly.

A little self-improvement will help you achieving success in your life. It may not look at the exact time, but these little changes do add up with time.

Goals

As you are changing your habits, you are equally focused on giving yourself some targets or goals. Where would you like to be in a year's or three or six years' time? It is not enough to have written down, instead visualize those goals. You goals should become second nature to you.

I have long term targets for myself. I am now very proficient at visualizing my goals that I now see certain details. For instance when I picture my dream home, I see blades of grass whenever I close my eyes and consider the yard and house I wish to own.

Do not feel frustrated if you cannot get this right the first time. Begin small and start visualizing.

The secret to successful goal setting is managing them. I was in the habit of setting some annual goals without achieving them. I began to dissect those goals into monthly goals.

Conclusion

Once you start to implement the steps outlined you will be able to change your life for the better. Good luck and enjoy!

www.ingramcontent.com/pod-product-compliance
Ingram Content Group UK Ltd.
Pitfield, Milton Keynes, MK11 3LW, UK
UKHW051845031025
8218UKWH00028B/288

9 780359 890361